Our Aim

Rook Publishing is committed to rediscovering historic, rare, and out-of-print books, and ensuring that such literary works are reproduced, so that they may be preserved for future generations.

Preserving the Past

Because we consider this work to have significant historic and cultural importance, we have made it available as part of our commitment to protect and preserve the world's literature in affordable, high quality, modern reproductions that remain true to the original work

This book is a facsimile reprint of a scarce and antiquarian book. Due the age and source of the original document, it may contain imperfections such as notations, marginalia, marks and other flaws within its pages.

I0776744

www.rookpublishing.co.uk

Ritual

~AND~

Book of Forms

OF THE ORDER

Sons of St. George.

As Adopted by the SUPREME LODGE

NEW YORK CITY,

OCTOBER 4TH, 1895.

ST. GEORGE JOURNAL,
126 North Ninth Street, Philadelphia.

Officers of Subordinate Lodges.

PRESIDENT,

VICE PRESIDENT,

SECRETARY,

TREASURER,

MESSENGER,

ASSISTANT SECRETARY,

ASSISTANT MESSENGER,

CHAPLAIN,

INSIDE SENTINEL,

OUTSIDE SENTINEL,

THREE TRUSTEES.

DIAGRAM OF LODGE ROOM.

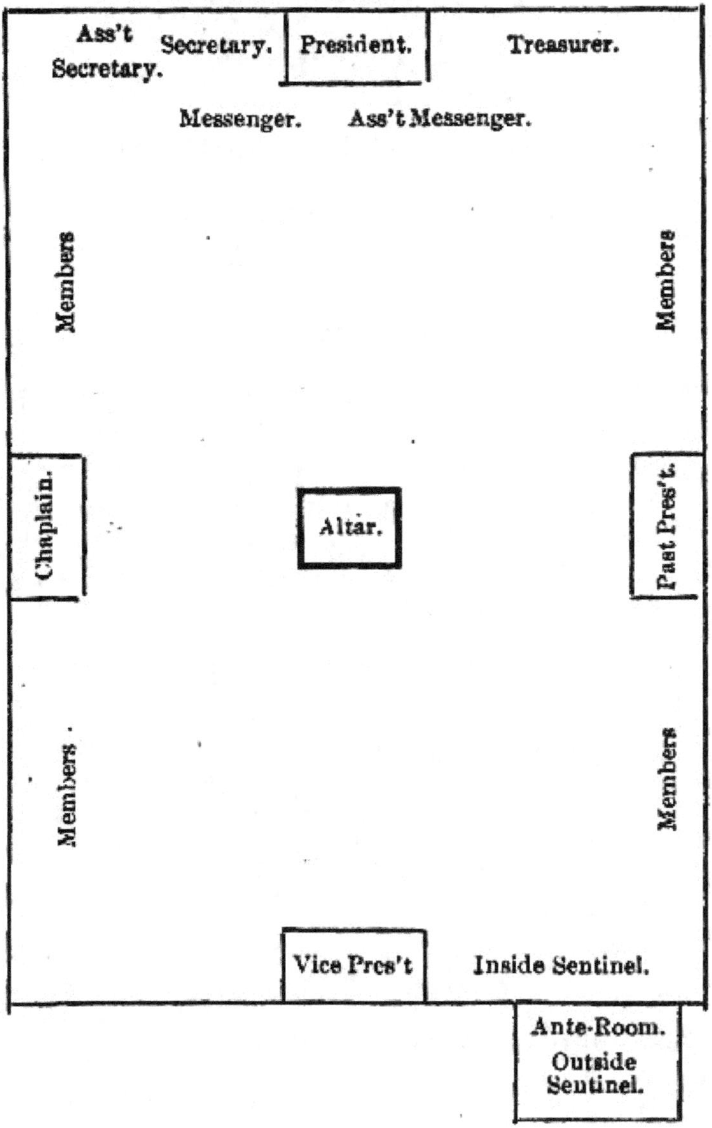

Opening : and : Closing.

OPENING OF THE LODGE.

W. P.—Officers and Brothers will clothe themselves in regalia. Officers take your stations. Inside Sentinel, notify Brothers in the ante-room to enter, and then secure the door. Worthy Messenger advance, give me the current password. See that all present are in possession of the same, and have on regalia of this degree.

W. M.—Worthy President, I find the Brothers correct.

(If any should be without the password, the W. M. will refer him to the W. P., who will give it to him if he is entitled to receive it.—Members must rise to their feet while giving the M. the password and grip.—No Brother will be allowed to pass between the Altar and Dais during the transaction of business.)

(*Call up officers.*)

W. P.—Inside Sentinel you will direct the Outside Sentinel to present himself, and you remain in his station until relieved.

O. S.—Worthy President, I report for duty.

W. P.—Brother Outside Sentinel your duty is to guard the outer door, upon you depends the privacy of this Lodge. You will retire to your station and relieve the Inside Sentinel.

[After the I. S. returns to his station the W. P. proceeds:]

W. P.—Worthy Vice President, what are the duties of your office?

W. V. P.—It is my duty to perform the ceremonies intrusted to me, to support the Worthy President in the discharge of his duties, assist him in maintaining order in the Lodge room, and appoint a minority of all committees, unless otherwise ordered by the Lodge.

W. P.—Worthy Secretary explain your duty.

W. S.—It is my duty to make and keep a true record of the proceedings of this Lodge; accurate accounts between the Lodge and its members; receive all monies, and pay the same over to the Worthy Treasurer, taking his receipt therefor.

W. P.—Your duty, Worthy Messenger?

W. M.—It is my duty to examine the Brothers prior to opening the Lodge, assist the

Worthy President and Worthy Vice President according to my office, and see that the Salutation sign is correctly given.

W. P.—Inside Sentinel, your duty!

I. S.—It is my duty to prove every Brother before he is admitted, and announce his name to the Worthy President.

(*Call up Lodge.*)

W. P.—Worthy Chaplain, please open our session with the Lord's Prayer.

W. C.—Let us pray:

Our Father, which art in Heaven, hallowed be thy name. Thy kingdom come. Thy will be done on earth as it is in Heaven. Give us this day our daily bread. And forgive us our trespasses, as we forgive those who tresspass against us. And lead us not into temptation; but deliver us from evil. For thine is the kingdom, and the power, and the glory, forever and ever. Amen.

W. P.—Brothers, let us sing our OPENING ODE:

[*After Ode is sung, turn over to page 8.*]

Opening Ode.

Tune, "Duke Street."
J. HATTON.

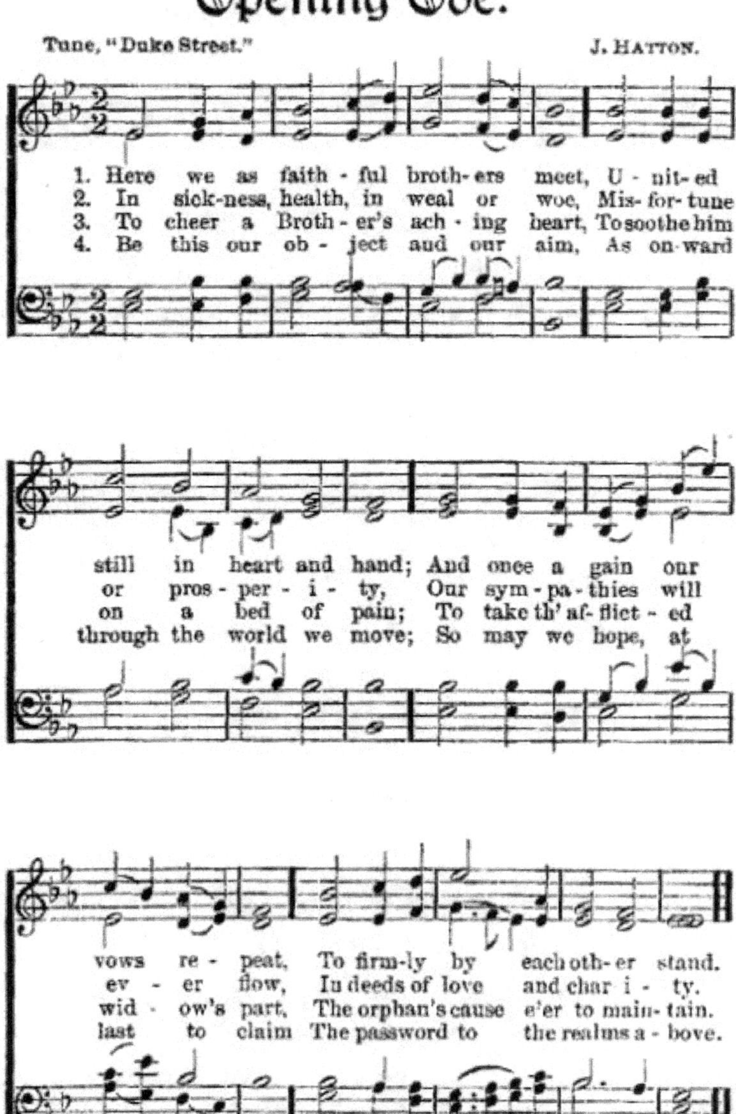

1. Here we as faith - ful broth- ers meet, U - nit- ed
2. In sick-ness, health, in weal or woe, Mis- for- tune
3. To cheer a Broth- er's ach - ing heart, To soothe him
4. Be this our ob - ject and our aim, As on-ward

still in heart and hand; And once a gain our
or pros - per - i - ty, Our sym - pa- thies will
on a bed of pain; To take th' af- flict - ed
through the world we move; So may we hope, at

vows re - peat, To firm-ly by each oth- er stand.
ev - er flow, In deeds of love and char i - ty.
wid - ow's part, The orphan's cause e'er to main- tain.
last to claim The password to the realms a - bove.

W. P.—Officers and Brothers, it is my duty to open this Lodge for the transaction of such business as may be legally brought before it. While we are together, let no animosity hold an influence over our hearts. No unseemly conduct or language mar the pleasure of our meeting. Unity of opinion cannot be expected upon all subjects, but the harmony of this Lodge will not be disturbed if the members will submit to the will of the majority. These principles and motives actuating us, we shall not fail in our objects—the advancement of our Order, and the welfare of all worthy Englishmen.

W. P.—Worthy Messenger, adjust the altar. Officers and Brothers, by virtue of my office I declare this Lodge legally open.

(*Call Down.*)

ORDER OF BUSINESS.

W. P.—Worthy Secretary, call the roll of officers.

W. P.—Worthy Secretary, read the minutes of our preceeding meeting. (*After the minutes are read.*) Brothers, the minutes just read, are the minutes of our last regular meeting. Is there anything omitted, or are there any corrections to be made? (*Pause*) If not I will declare them approved.

W. P.—We will now hear excuses of officers absent at our last meeting.

W. P.—Do any know of a Brother sick or in distress?

W. P.—Any report from our Relief Committee or Physician?

W. P.—Worthy Secretary, "Reports of Investigating Committees" are now in order.

[If there be any, they must be read in open session by the Worthy Secretary, and if reported favorably by Committee and Physician, be balloted for.]

W. P.—Worthy Messenger prepare the ballot box.

[When prepared, show it to the Worthy President and Worthy Vice President, by exposing the empty side, then place it on the altar.]

W. P.—Brothers, you will cast your ballot for Mr . . . ., for initiation in this Lodge. He has been favorably reported upon by the Committee and Physician. Form in single file in front of the altar, facing the dais. White balls elect. Black cubes (*or balls*) reject. I now declare the ballot open.

W. P.—Have all voted who wish? If so, I declare the ballot closed. Worthy Messenger, display the ballot box to the Vice President, then bring it to me for inspection.

W. P.—Worthy Vice President how find you the ballot?

W. V. P.—Favorable to the candidate.

(If three black cubes (or balls) appear, the Worthy Vice President will say "unfavorable;" the Worthy President will then order another ballot, (which shall be taken forthwith), and if unfavorable, the Worthy President will declare the candidate rejected.)

W. P.—Favorable here. I therefore declare
Mr. . . . . . duly elected for initiation in this
Lodge.

Inside Sentinel, inquire of Outside Sentinel if
any candidates are in waiting. If so, their names.

I. S.—Worthy President, there is in waiting
Mr. . . . . . .

INITIATION OF CANDIDATES.

W. P.—The Worthy Secretary and the Worthy
Messenger will retire to the ante-room, and ascer-
tain if there are any candidates in waiting. If so,
propound the necessary questions, collect the balance of the fee, and report.

[Worthy Secretary and Worthy Messenger approach the
Altar, salute and retire.]

W. M.—Mr. . . . . have you made and
signed an application to become a member of this
Lodge of the Order Sons of St. George?

(Candidate answers.)

W. M.—And are the statements therein con-
tained, true to the best of your knowledge and
belief?

(Candidate answers.)

W. M.—In seeking admission, is it your desire
to co-operate with your fellow countrymen, and thus
advance that Fraternal, Social, and Beneficial intercourse with each other, which are the chief objects
of our organization?

(Candidate answers.)

W. M.—Will you endeavor to live up to its
principles to the best of your ability, and to
comply with the requirements of the Constitution

and the By-Laws of this Lodge?

(Candidate answers.)

[The Worthy Secretary will now collect the balance of the fees, and with the Worthy Messenger, will return to the Lodge room, approach the Altar, salute and report.]

W. P.—Worthy Messenger, you will retire and prepare the candidate for initiation.

(When there are more than one candidate, the plural will be used, and the language changed accordingly.)

[Worthy Messenger salutes and retires to the ante-room, where he places the belt around the candidate's waist; blindfolds him then approaching the inner door, gives * * * raps.]

W. I. S.—Who knocks at our inner gate?

W. M.—A Stranger who desires admittance to membership in our beloved Order.

W. I. S.—By what right does he ask such a favor?

W. M.—By being of proper parentage and in full sympathy with our aims and objects.

W. I. S.—Is he aware that only those who faithfully perform the duties of Life are admitted?

W. M.—He is.

W. I. S.—Is he properly prepared?

W. M.—He is.

W. I. S.—Has he the password?

W. M.—He has not, but from credentials that he bears I will vouch for him.

W. I. S.—Worthy President; there is without, a stranger, not in possession of the password, but, who is accompanied and vouched for by a Brother Knight, the Worthy Messenger.

W. P.—Being so excellently vouched for, in the name of God and St. George, I bid him enter.

[Worthy President calls up the Lodge, and all sing the INITIATION ODE.

Initiation Ode.

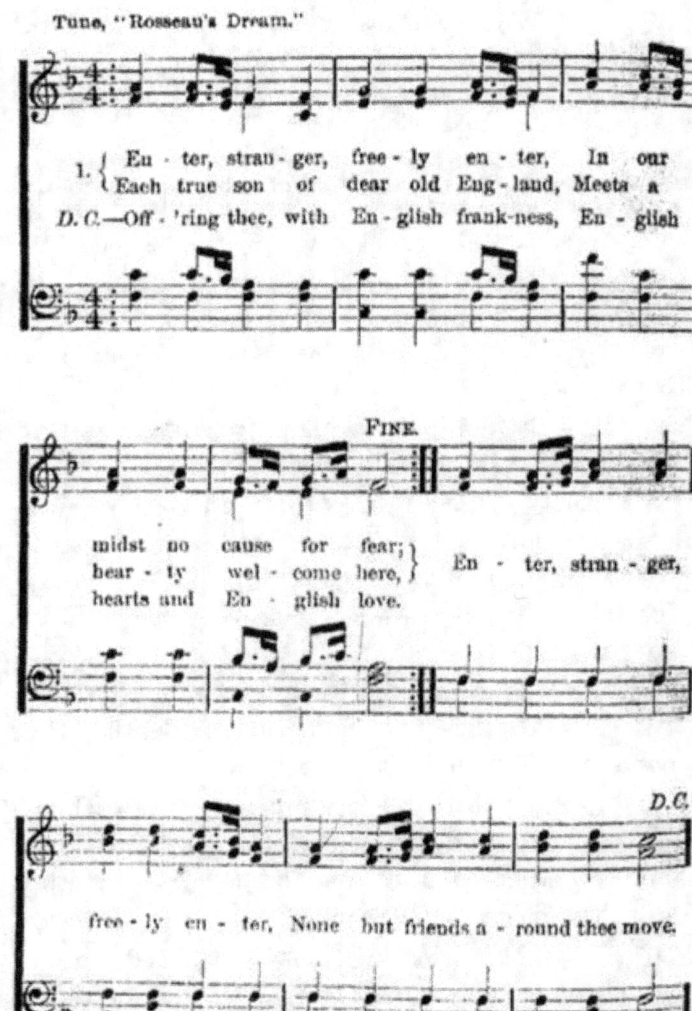

W. M.—Worthy Vice President; I have the
pleasure of introducing to you a Stranger who is
desirous of being admitted into our honorable Order.
He has passed the inner gate, and awaits your
pleasure.

W. V. P.—'Tis well, you will continue your
journey stopping at the Altars of Fraternity, Concord and Love; where the Stranger will be instructed in the principles of our Order.

(Worthy Messenger leading candidate by the arm toward
the station of the Worthy Past President, and timing himself
to the music, repeats these words:)

W. M.—The motto of a Son of St. George is
Fraternity, Concord and Love. In our devotion to
them we have erected Altars to their honor.

(By this time he should have reached the station of the
Worthy Past President, halting, he addresses that officer as
follows:)

W. M.—Worthy Past President, I present to
you a candidate whom I have reason to believe will
bow to the shrine of Fraternity.

W. P. P.—My Friend, you are now on the
threshold of the Altar of Fraternity. It is my
privilege to instruct you in its meaning. Fraternity, the first word of the motto of the Sons of St.
George, is a leading feature of the natural instincts
of man. It begins with his early years, is nurtured
through youth and manhood to old age, and ends
only with his death. The question may be asked

has this fraternizing propensity of man, been of any practical benefit to his fellows? We answer, Yes. In all civilized nations where this feature has been encouraged, it has resulted in the upbuilding of those institutions whose object is the practical recognition of the Universal Brotherhood of Man.

Such my friend, is the aim and object of this noble Order, to which you have made application for membership.

Are you willing to practice this virtue in entering into membership with us?

(*Candidate Answers.*)

W. P. P.—'Tis well, Worthy Messenger and Friend, proceed on your journey.

W. M.—(*To candidate, timing his words as before*) We will journey on to the next station where we expect to gain further knowledge of the principles of the Order. We have now arrived at the Altar of Concord. * *Rap.*

W. P.—Worthy Messenger, whom have we here?

W. M.—Worthy President, I have in charge a friend, who is desirous of being further instructed in the principles of our Order.

W. P.—Has he been duly instructed at the Altar of Fraternity?

W. M.—He has.

W. P.—My Friend, what has been said of Fraternity, applies also to Concord. Concord is harmony, and without it no Fraternity can long exist. This is not however so easy to practice, because man's natural tendency, when opposed is to fight, by force of arms or by force of words; and either may give sharp wounds to body or mind, and fraternal feeling thus be destroyed.

The highest civilization exists not where right is sustained by armed force, but where rights are adjusted by friendly arbitration.

In your intercourse with us will you endeavor to cultivate this quality which makes for peace?

(*Candidate Answers.*)

W. P.—Worthy Messenger pass on with your charge to the Altar of Love.

(The Worthy Messenger will time his walk as before repeating as follows:)

We have yet one more station to reach before we arrive at our journey's end, there we will no doubt receive that full instruction, which will carry us safely through.

[Halts in front of the Worthy Chaplain, who raps, and says:]

Worthy Chaplain, I take pleasure in introducing to you a friend, who has been instructed at the Altars of Fraternity and Concord, and now having arrived at the Altar of Love, desires to learn from your lips the knowledge of that divine light, that will illumine and make light his earthly journey to its end.

W. C.—My Friend, the last of the trio of words adopted by our Order, is one that appeals more than any other to the moral nature of man.

It embraces all that is claimed for Fraternity and
Concord, but in a much greater degree. Love is
an affection of the heart, excited by that which
commands our admiration. Self sacrifice and devotion to others, are the teachings of this virtue, and
its aim is to carry into effect, that which was com-
manded nearly nineteen hundred years ago. "To
love the Lord thy God with all thy heart, and
thy neighbor as thy self." In the perfect realization
of that command, lies the justification of fraternal organization, which should never cease to exist
as long as time shall last, until then;

> "Let mutual joys our mutual love combine,
> And love, and love born confidence be
> [thine."]

Having been fully instructed in the principles
of Fraternity, Concord and Love, are you in sympathy with their teachings?

(*Candidate Answers.*)

W. C.—'Tis well, Worthy Messenger, conduct
the candidate to his journey's end.

[Proceeds to station of Worthy Vice President.]

W. M.—Worthy Vice President, I present to
you a candidate who has been fully instructed
at our Altars, and is desirous of proceeding to
his journey's end.

W. V. P.—My Friend, we have admitted you
thus far because of good report, being of proper
parentage, and having declared yourself in sympathy with our objects, you desire to unite with

us of kindred blood in the bonds of harmony by the golden chain of nationality; thus giving to each other the benefits of association, helping to promote each other's interests in life, giving relief in distress, aid and sympathy when sick, comfort and advice to your loved ones when you are gone, and when the final summons shall come such substantial sympathy, as shall lift the survivors above the unfeeling charity of the world.

This Order is not intended to inculcate love for the Mother Country, at the expense of your loyalty to the Country of your adoption. It is not that we love Old England the less, but our adopted Country the more, yet only because of its greater opportunity for the advancement of mankind. No true Englishman or man of English blood can ever be a traitor, either to his own or the country of his adoption.

With your religious or political faith we do not interfere, leaving you free to act as your conscience may dictate. But you will be required to give our laws faithful observance, obedience to our officers, and prompt payments of dues and assessments, as otherwise in sickness or death your family would suffe:, thereby forfeiting all rights to benefits of any nature whatever. We also expect that you will use your influence to extend our Order and watch over the welfare of our Brothers.

But before you can join us, and participate in our privileges, you will be required to take the solemn obligation of the Sons of St. George. This obligation, though binding in its character

and lifelong in its duration, will not in anyway
lower your self esteem, or interfere with your
duties to your family, your country or your God;
with these assurances on our part are you willing
to proceed ?

(*Candidate Answers.*)

Worthy Messenger, conduct the candidate to
to the Altar, that he may receive the obligation.

W. P.—Worthy Assistant Messenger, you will
assist the Worthy Messenger, while the Worthy
Chaplain is administering the obligation

[After the Worthy Messenger has placed the candidate
in position, kneeling, the Worthy Messenger and Worthy
Assistant Messenger, cross swords over the head of the candidate and remain in that position until the obligation is finish-
ed. Meanwhile the Sir Knights will assemble and form the
Shield facing inwards, with left index finger pointing upwards
right hand on next Brother's shoulder, and thus remain until
orders from the Worthy President. The Worthy Chaplain
having advanced to the Altar in front of candidate, proceeds
as follows:]

W. C.—Place your right hand on the Holy
Bible, Sword and Shield of St. George. Raise your
left hand, with your index finger pointing upwards,
and repeat after me:

I . . . . in the name of God and St.
George, and in the presence of these Brethren here
assembled, do solemnly and sincerely promise without any mental reservation whatever, that under
any and all circumstances in which I may be placed,
I will never reveal the secret work of this Order.

I will keep inviolate, all signs, passwords, and tokens
of this Order, excepting it be when giving instruction in the course of duty, or to an officer properly authorized to demand and receive the same.
I also promise to faithfully uphold the Constitution and laws of the Supreme Lodge, and the
Grand Lodge of this Grand Jurisdiction as well as the
By-Laws of this Lodge.

I especially promise not to write on anything
movable or immovable, any of the secret work of
this Order by which it may become known to the
outer world.

I will to the extent of my ability relieve a
Brother in distress, warn him of any danger,
visit him when sick, obey the Laws of the Order
and the officers of this Lodge.

I further promise, not to engage in any dis-
cussion of a religious or political nature during
the session of this Lodge, nor allow others to do
so, I make these pledges upon my honor as a
man with full knowledge of their responsibility
and will ever be faithful in the performance of
the same.

[Members will now sing the OBLIGATION ODE.]

Obligation Ode.

W. C.—Let us pray, Almighty God and Supreme Ruler of the Universe and the preserver of us all. Wilt thou look down and guide this Brother who has just promised to be true and faithful to us in the bonds of Fraternity, Concord and Love. Sustain him with thine arm in the hour of danger, give him safe reliance and a firm trust in thee, that he may prove a true and Worthy Knight and ever after be faithful to our principles and to thee.

All respond, Amen.

[W. M. here removes the hoodwink from candidate.]

W. C.—Worthy Messenger, you will conduct the Brother to the Worthy Vice President, who will invest him with the Garter.

W. V. P.—Brother, I now invest you with this emblem of Knighthood, wear it proudly, and as need requires that you step forward in any good work or cause, may it remind you of the earnest devotion, you should give to any cause, when once espoused; provided always that it be the cause of truth and right. Place your left foot on this stool and repeat after me:

I . . . . herewith offer up my petition to the Supreme Ruler of us all, that He may so guide my steps aright, as to bring no disgrace upon this emblem, this honorable band of blue.

[The Worthy Messenger will invest the candidate with the Garter while he is repeating the above.]

W. V. P.—Worthy Messenger, you will now conduct the Brother to our Worthy Past President who will invest him with the Sword of Knighthood.

W. P. P.—Brother, I will now place within your care and keeping, this Sword, and while in your possession, may it inspire you with its emblematical virtues of Firmness, Justice and Truth. Its hilt is symbolical of firmness, which is essentially necessary for us to possess in order to combat and conquer the trials and difficulties of life and to live up to our obligations under the stress of temptation.

Its blade is symbolical of that evenly balanced justice which should be the rule of action in our intercourse with our Brethren in all the relations of our earthly life.

The point of its blade being endowed with truth is symbolical of that cause in which it can only be drawn with honor; truth and honor being dearer than life to a Son of St. George.

[Hands sword to Candidate. Worthy Messenger adjusts it to his belt.]

Worthy Messenger you will conduct the Brother to our Worthy Chaplain who will invest him with the Badge of our Order.

W. C.—Brother, it is with pleasure that I invest you with the Badge of our Order, (*Hands Badge to the Worthy Messenger who adjusts it.*)

This Badge when on your breast should be to you the outward sign of Knightly courtesy within. The highest Knightly courtesy bids us to believe no ill of a brother Knight, but always to view the words and deeds of our Brethren in the most favorable light. You can keep this Golden Rule of Knighthood ever in your mind by remembering the motto inscribed thereon (Honi Soit Qui Mal y Pense) which translated means "Evil be to him who evil thinks."

Worthy Messenger, conduct the Brother to the Worthy President, inform him that he has been duly invested with the arms and insignia of Knighthood, instructed in the lessons they teach, and now awaits his Knightly commands that bid him rise an equal Knight within these walls.

W. M.—Worthy President, before you stands Brother . . . . who seeks from you the fullest honor of a Knight, which only your decree can give; he has been fully instructed at our several stations, and I recommend him to your kind consideration.

W. P.—My Brother, it becomes my duty as Worthy President of this Lodge, to give you such further instructions as will enable you to properly fulfil the duties, which you have now assumed by your obligation.

As you have learned, the words of a Son of St. George, are, "Fraternity, Concord and Love," the initials of which, F., C. and L., you may use when addressing a communication to one of your Brethren.

The grip is given thus . . . . The position of the fingers represents the Cross of St. George, and is intended to remind you of your duty to the Brotherhood, and the necessity for our general prosperity, of going hand in hand together through this life.

The salutation sign is given thus . . . . The placing of the . . . . thus, is intended to remind us of the obligation we have all taken. Raising the . . . . thus, to impress upon you the absolute necessity of forever keeping secret all that transpires in the Lodge room, and returning the . . . thus, is the open hand of fellowship which you offer to all worthy Brothers.

The salute in honor of a visit by a Grand Lodge Officer (when announced as such) is given thus . . . .

The salute in honor of a visit by a Supreme Lodge officer (when announced as such) is given thus . . . .

We have a voting sign which is made in this manner. . . .

In order to prove yourself a member of our Order we have a recognition sign with its answer, and for your instruction I will exemplify these signs with our Worthy Messenger. Should you be outside of a Lodge, and wish to know if there are any Sons of St. George present, you will make this sign . . . . Should it be observed by a Brother, he will answer you by making this sign . . . . . You will then approach him and say . . . . . He will say . . . . . And you will say . . . . Then, to make the test complete you will extend your hand and allow him to give you the grip, which, if correct, you will return. Should it be in the night season or at any time or situation when the signs cannot be seen, you will say . . . . . Should this be heard by any

Brother, he will answer . . . . . . and at once hasten to you.

Should you be in distress or need immediate pecuniary assistance, you will use this sign . . . When a Brother gives this sign, it is your duty if you upon examination, find him worthy, to render what assistance you can without material injury to yourself or family, as you never know the moment a similar misfortune may overtake you.

I will instruct you how to gain admittance to a Lodge of this Order. If the Lodge is not in session, you will clothe yourself in proper regalia enter the room and take your seat.

If the Lodge is in session you will approach the outer door and give such an alarm as will attract the attention of the Outside Sentinel. He will raise the wicket and you will give him the first half of the current password, which is . . . . You will then be admitted to the ante-room where you will clothe yourself in accordance with your rank advance to the inner door where you will . . . . If your alarm is returned you will know there is business before the Lodge and you must wait its conclusion. When the wicket is raised by the Inside Sentinel you will give your name, and the name and number of your Lodge, in this way: Brother . . . . of . . . . . Lodge, No. . . (that being the name and number of this Lodge.) Or if in your own Lodge, you will say: Brother . . . . of this Lodge. You will also give the second half of the password, which is . . . . You will be admitted and must at once proceed to the front of the Altar, facing the Worthy

President and salute in this manner . . . . .The
Worthy President will return in the same way
when you may be seated. Should you forget the
password you will so report to the Sentinels and
upon being admitted you will salute the Worthy
President and before taking your seat present
yourself to the Worthy President who will give
you the password if you are entitled to receive
it.

Should you wish to retire while the Lodge
is in session, you will approach the Altar and
give the salute, if returned by the Worthy President
you may retire.

I will explain to you the use of the gavel.
. . . . Commands order in the Lodge room and
seats the Lodge when standing . . . . the officers
will rise . . . . the entire Lodge will rise.

Worthy Messenger you will place the Brother
in position to receive the high honor of
Knighthood.

.[Candidate kneels with right knee on stool, the Worthy
President steps down in front of Candidate and
says:]

By virtue of the trust reposed and power in
me vested by my Brother Knights, I now invest
you with the Degree of Knighthood, and with
this good sword I dub thee Knight in the name
of God, (*Taps Knight with sword*) our Country (*taps
again*) and St. George (*Taps*) rise Sir Knight . .
. .

Worthy Messenger you will present the Brother
to our Worthy Past President for his examination.

(Seats Lodge.)

W. M.—Worthy Past President, I have the honor to introduce to you our newly initiated Brother . . . .

W. P. P.—It is with pleasure I welcome you to our Order and this Lodge. You have been fully informed as to the objects and principles of this order, as you advance in our confidence and esteem, you will more fully realize the benefits to be derived from this association, whose strongest tie is that of kindred blood. The beauties of our beloved Order are most truly expressed in our trio of words; Fraternity, Concord and Love, the principles and teachings of which have been fully explained to you. Resolve then, my Brother, henceforth to practice these virtues of Fraternity, Concord and Love. I will now examine you in the signs, grips and passwords to see if you understand them.

[Examines candidate and continues.]

With the work now in your possession, you will be able to make yourself known anywhere, as a member of the Order, Sons of St. George.

Worthy Messenger, you will conduct our worthy Brother to the Worthy Secretary, that he may sign his name to our Constitution and thence proceed to the Worthy President, to await his commands.

[Candidate signs Constitution and is then taken to the station of Worthy President.]

Welcome Ode.

Tune, "To The West."

1. Here's the grip; Brother, take it! 'Tis an Englishman's grasp,
2. Here's the grip; Brother, take it! 'Tis a Brit- on's true sign,

With the pledge of   his   hon- or, As thy hand he doth clasp;
That his heart goes   out   with it   To   min- gle with thine;

'Tis the promise   he gives thee, That, true to   his creed,
Then take, and   re - turn it, Where - ev - er you be,

He will help a   true Broth-er   In time of his need.
To   each "Son of St. George," That may give it to thee.

W. P.—Worthy Messenger, you will retire
with the newly-made Brother, and work your
way into the Lodge.

[They retire, re-enter, salute and remain standing at the
Altar.]

W. P.—[*Calls up Lodge*.] Brother Sir Knights,
I have the pleasure of introducing to you Brother
. . . . I commend him to your good offices.
Let us give him the grip.

[Officers advance and greet the candidate with the grip,
meanwhile the Sir Knights sing the WELCOME ODE.]

W. P.—I now declare a recess of . . . minutes,
in which to welcome with fraternal courtesy our
newly-made Brother.

[The regular order of business will then be resumed.]

W. P.—Reports of Committees by seniority.

W. P.—Proposals for membership are now in
order.

[If any, receive in proper form; appoint committees.]

W. P.—Payment of dues.

[The W. P. may in his discretion, declare a recess for a
few minutes during payment of dues. When the time is up
gavel for order, and resume business.]

W. P.—Worthy Secretary are there any com-
munications?

[If any, they must be read; receive them in proper form,
when necessary dispose of them in New Business.]

W. P.—Payment of bills.

W. P.—Unfinished business.

W. P.—New business.

W. P.—Receipts of the evening.

[W. A. S. or W. S. will read out names and amounts paid, so that mistakes, if any, may be rectified.]

W. P.—Good and Welfare.

[This is the proper time to introduce something, which will make the meetings interesting, and be calculated to draw a better attendance. Strive to have these entertainments intellectual and amusing.]

CLOSING.

[Call up. The Closing Ode may be sung here or dispensed with, at the option of the W. P.]

W. P.—Worthy Messenger, dismantle the Altar, secure our Rituals, collect all Lodge property.

[The Worthy Messenger dismantles the Altar, salutes, when the Worthy President proceeds.]

W. P.—Sir Knights, I now declare this Lodge closed, and bid you to retire in Faith, Hope and Love.—Faith in our principles, hope in their future, and a love for our cause.

[*One rap of gavel.*]

Closing Ode.

Tune, "Auld Lang Syne."

1. And now, the hour once more has come When, Brothers, we must part;
2. 'Till link'd fast by the gold-en chain Of love and sympathy,

Let us re-mem-ber, ev-'ry one, The cause we have at heart.
A might-y band of Brotherhood, St. George's Sons will be.

God pros-per still our glorious cause, And bless the grand design,
Thus, as we give our parting word, Once more our vows we plight,

Till Brit-ons, in fra-ter-nal love, Their hands together join.
To live in peace and har-mo-ny—Good night, good night, good night!

INSTALLATION OF OFFICERS

This Ceremony may be made Public, if desired.

[The Worthy Grand President or his Deputy and District Grand Messenger will visit the Lodge on the night of Installation, and after being received with the honors due their station, will, at the proper time, present themselves at the altar, salute the W. P., who calls up]

W. G. P.—Worthy President, we are here to install your officers for the ensuing term. Have they been constitutionally elected? Are they clear on the books and free from charges?

W. P.—Worthy Grand President, the officers-elect have been legally elected, are clear on our books and free from charges. I now cordially invite you to the chair.

[The W. G. P. and Messenger will advance, and the W. G. P. will take the chair, the W. P. standing to his right, with gavel in hand, will then say:]

W. P.—Officers and Brethren, before surrendering my gavel, the symbol of my authority, to our Worthy Grand President, I feel that I must thank the Officers and Brethren for the many kindnesses and courtesies extended to me while occupying this Chair, and I sincerely hope and trust that my term of service has not lessened the confidence and respect reposed in me when you so kindly elected me your presiding officer. Worthy Grand President, into your hands I place the gavel, books and charter, hoping my successor whom you are about to install, will be blessed

with health and strength to faithfully perform
the trust reposed in him, and that the Lodge
will be prosperous under his administration.

[W. G. P., calls down, the Worthy President then takes
a seat to the right of W. G. P.]

W. G. P.—Worthy Secretary, please favor me
with a list of the officers-elect. The *elected* officers
for the term now ended will please vacate their
chairs and surrender to the Worthy Grand Messenger their regalia and all Lodge property now
in their possession. Worthy President, you will
now please take your seat as Junior Past Worthy
President. Worthy Grand Messenger conduct the
the Past President to his chair.

Worthy Grand Messenger, conduct the Worthy
President, Vice President and Messenger elect, to
ante-room. examine them as to their qualification
for the offices to which they have been elected
and be sure they understand thoroughly the secret
work of our Order.

[The W. G. M., and officers elect named, salute,
retire, and after examination will return, salute, and the
W. G. M., will report if he finds them correct, as follows:]

W. G. M.—Worthy Grand President, I have
examined the officers-elect and found them quali-
fied and well versed in the secret work of our
Order.

W. G. P.—Worthy Grand Messenger, place
the officers-elect in position in front of the Dais
the Worthy President at my right, and the others
according to their rank.

[When all are standing before the W. G. P., he will say:]

My Brothers, the duties connected with each
of the offices to which you have been elected
are plainly and forcibly laid down for your guid-
ance in the Subordinate Lodge Constitution, which
I will now read, that you may not plead ignor-
ance of that which is required of you.

[Reads the duties of each elected officer and then says:]

Having been instructed in your several duties,
do you each accept the office to which you have
been elected?

Answer.—I do.

W. G. P.—'Tis well. (*Call up.*)

Place your right hand on your left breast,
raise your left hand, with the index finger pointing upwards, and repeat after me:

I do solemnly promise to perform the duties
of the office to which I have been elected, as
laid down in the Constitution and Laws of the
Order Sons of St. George, and the By-Laws of
this Lodge, to the best of my ability, also to
study the rules, the regulations, and the work of
the ceremonies of Initiation, as laid down in the
Ritual; and to do all in my power, by punctual
attendance at our regular meetings, to promote
the best interests of this Lodge and the Order in
general. I make this pledge upon my honor as
a Son of St. George.

[Sing OBLIGATION ODE.]

W. G. P.—Worthy Grand Messenger, invest
them with the badges of their office and conduct
them to their several stations; the Trustee to a

seat in the body of the Lodge, first, and the rest according to their office, commencing with the Worthy Assistant Secretary, and the Worthy President last.

CHARGE OF THE W. G. P.

W. G. P.—Worthy President, before I deliver into your keeping, the Charter, and books pertaining to your office, it becomes my duty to warn you to avoid reading or rehearsing any part of the work of this Order before or in the hearing of any person not a member; you must not print or write, or allow to be printed or written, any of the secret work of our Order. Keep the Rituals in your own care, and deliver these books to none but a Grand Lodge officer or deputy.

Having full confidence in your integrity, I now present you with the Charter, books, copy of the Laws of the Order, and lastly, the gavel, the symbol of your authority, and heartily greet you [*here shake hands*] as Worthy President of . . . . Lodge, and hope you may have health and strength to fill the important position you now occupy.

Brethren of . . . . Lodge, No. . . . . Order Sons of St. George, I . . . . by the powers vested in me by the Grand Lodge of our beloved Order, do declare the officers of . . . . . Lodge, No. . . . duly and legally installed for the term.

[W. P. seats his Lodge and then proceeds to appoint his subordinate officers.]

SUBORDINATE OFFICERS.

W. P.—Brethren, I appoint for this term the following named subordinate officers:

For Worthy Assistant Messenger, Brother . . . . Brother . . . . , do you accept the office?

For Worthy Chaplain, Brother . . . . . . Brother . . . . . , do you accept the office?

For Worthy Inside Sentinel, Brother . . . . . Brother . . . . , do you accept the office?

For Worthy Outside Sentinel, Brother . . . . . Brother . . . . , do you accept the office?

Worthy Messenger, present them for Installation.

W. M.—Worthy President, I present to you for installation the subordinate officers for this term.

CHARGE OF W. P.

WORTHY ASSISTANT MESSENGER.

W. P.—Worthy Assistant Messenger, your duty is to assist the Worthy Messenger in opening and closing the Lodge, assist at the Initiation of Candidates, provide for the comfort of the Brethren, see that all Brothers properly salute when entering or retiring, and do all in your power to help do the work of the Lodge.

WORTHY CHAPLAIN.

W. P.—Worthy Chaplain, your duties are of a reverential nature, and you will open the

Lodge with prayer, and assist in such ceremonies as are required of you by the Ritual.

WORTHY INSIDE SENTINEL.

W. P.—Worthy Inside Sentinel, it is your duty to prove every Brother before admitting him, report all irregularities to the Worthy President, see that all Brothers are properly clothed, and allow none to enter without the password.

WORTHY OUTSIDE SENTINEL.

W. P.—Worthy Outside Sentinel, your duties are in the ante-room, upon the strict and faithful performance of your duties depends the privacy of this Lodge, you will see that no person enters who cannot prove himself, according to the rules and regulations of our Order; you must keep the outer door secure against improper intrusion, and submit all cases where you have a doubt to the Inside Sentinel, to be reported to the Worthy President for his action.

W. P.—Worthy Messenger, clothe the officers in regalia of office, and conduct them to their respective stations.

[The W. P. may in his discretion, resume business, or declare a recess; of course, if it is a public Installation, the business must all be done previous to the ceremony, and conclude with the CLOSING ODE.]

VISITATIONS.

[When a Supreme, Grand Lodge Officer, or visiting Brothers in a body, announce themselves to the Inside Sentinel, he will report the same to the W. P., who shall direct the Junior P. W. P. to retire and introduce them; on entering the W. P. calls up, and after the Salutation the P. W. P. shall say:]

P. W. P.—Worthy President, I have the honor of introducing to you . . . .

W. P.—In the name of this Lodge, permit me to tender you a hearty welcome, and to hope that your visit may prove a pleasure to you, and a profit to us.   (*Call Down.*)

[If a W. P. or a P. W. P., Grand or Supreme Lodge officer, the W. P. shall invite to the Dais. If the visitor be a Supreme or Grand Lodge officer, or a D. D. W. G. P., and announces himself as such, when he reaches the Dais, the W. P. shall call up and say:]

Officers and Brethren, I take great pleasure in introducing our Supreme (or Worthy Grand) . . . . . ; we will now honor him with the Supreme (or Grand Lodge) salute.

(*All salute.*)

And now, Supreme (or Worthy Grand) . . . permit me to resign into your hand the gavel of this Lodge.

[The Supreme or Grand Lodge officer will accept the gavel, and after a few appropriate remarks, return it to the W. P., who will then call down.]

FORM OF

Instituting New Lodges.

[The Instituting officers and staff will take their stations, as in the opening of a Subordinate Lodge, request all the applicants for Charter, who are not members of the Order to retire, and then open in usual form; after the Charter members are initiated, the Instituting officer will say:

W. G. P.—Brethren, we are assembled here
to fulfil an interesting and pleasing duty, that of
creating a new branch of our beloved Order, and
I hope and trust that you all will find association with us to be of such great advantage social-
ly, morally and materially, that you will never
have cause to regret having joined this Order;
but, on the contrary, will be so well pleased as
to lose no opportunity to induce others to follow
you, and thus strengthen and extend our aims,
objects and good influences. Although it should
be the aim of every Lodge to increase its membership, let me impress upon you to be very
careful in introducing individuals for membership
in our beloved Order, of whom you, in your
inward heart, have a doubt. In fact, your best
guide is, to recommend no man whom you will
not be willing afterward to welcome in your own
home, and introduce to your family. New Lodges
are inclined to be a little careless in this matter,
but it should not be so. One unworthy man
admitted to membership, may cause you to lose
many who would have made desirable members and
been a benefit to your Lodge. And to you who
may hereafter, or perhaps to night be appointed on
investigating committees, I would say, it is your
duty, not so much to visit the candidate, although
this is requisite, as it is to thoroughly inquire into
his mode of life, and general reputation for probity,
morality and respectability.

And now, my Brethren, let me advise you that
in all your discussions and differences of opinion,
which you are sure to have, that you never forget

to treat each other with due respect. We all have
ideas of our own, and it is only manly to express
them, but in so doing, let us avoid all sarcasm,
irony, personalities, and ungenerous remarks, and
when beaten fairly, give graciously in, always remembering that one or the other must lose their
point.

I will now call upon the Worthy Grand
Secretary to read the Charter, under which you
will have the privilege of working so long as you
comply with its requirements and the laws of our
Order.

(*W. G. S. reads Charter.*)

And now Brethren, before you elect your
officers, I would charge you to elect, as officers
of this Lodge, none but those you believe to be
thoroughly competent to fill the same, and let no
one accept either a position as an officer, or on
a committee, unless you feel that you are competent, and have the necesssary time to discharge
the duties of the same. Ambition is laudable,
aim high and you certainly will not strike low;
do whatever you have to do thoroughly well,
rest on your merits, and your success is certain;
and, lastly, let me impress all with the fact that,
to be successful, you must always bow to the will
of the majority; follow this, you will be prosperous, and harmony your constant guest. I now
declare nomination and election of officers in order.

[At conclusion of which, install, as per regular ceremony,
and then say :]

Officer and Brothers, by the authority in me
vested as . . . . . , I declare . . . . . Lodge, No.
. . . . , duly and legally instituted a Lodge of
the Order, Sons of St. George.

FUNERAL CEREMONY.

[The Lodge shall assemble at the regular place of meeting
punctually at the time called, and open in regular form. The
Worthy President will appoint a Marshall and Assistant, the
Brethren will put on Funeral Regalia, white gloves and a sprig
of evergreen; the Worthy President will then close the Lodge
and the Brethren will form in procession, and pass from the
room to the place where the deceased Brother is to be taken.
The order of procession will be as follows, two by two:]

[FIRST.—Past Worthy Presidents;]

[SECOND.—Officers of the Lodge;]

[THIRD.—Members.]

[When they arrive at the house they will open ranks and
permit the body to be carried through to the hearse, after
which they will close ranks and march to the front of hearse,
members, officers, P. W. P's. last. Upon arriving at Church
or cemetery, ranks are broken and the body and mourners
pass through the ranks, then the officers will fall in and pass
through, and the members in due form. Arriving at grave
the W. P. will stand at head and Chaplain at foot, and the
officers and members in as good order as the nature of the
grounds will admit. After the performance of the religious
ceremony and before the closing of the grave, the W. P. will
deliver the following:]

W. P.—BRETHREN AND FRIENDS:—We are
assembled to render the last office the living may
minister to the dead, the last act we perform for
a departed Brother. We do not assemble to benefit the deceased, but rather to impress upon the

minds of surviving friends the necessity of preparing to meet the summons when it shall be our turn to cancel the debt we owe to nature. "Man is born to die." The decree of Heaven is, "Dust thou art, and unto dust thou shall return." We must all wait the inevitable hour. What is our life? "It is even a vapor that appeareth for a little time and then vanisheth away." Where are the myriads of the human family who have lived and figured on the earth? "They are asleep with their fathers, and the place that once knew them shall know them no more for ever."

Oh, let us, then, reflect and be prepared for the change which awaits us all. Death comes when least expected, and spares none. He calls for youth in its harmlessness and innocency, manhood in its vigor and prime, and old age, tottering and decrepit. My Brethren, we are too easily dazzled with the pursuits, pleasures and wealth of this world. Although hardly a day passes but we see or hear of disaster, accident or death, yet how seldom do we think of our own mortality. Often we are called upon to follow our fellow-men to the grave, yet we immediately return to the world, heedless, perhaps, of the precarious tenure of life and the certainty of that end to which all flesh is rapidly tending; the living of to-day may be the dead of to-morrow, "for we appear and disappear like the waves of the sea" "In the midst of life we are in death." Death is no respector of persons; all must bow, rich and poor, weak and strong, the lowest beg-

gar and the king on the throne—all are levelled
by Death.

Brethren, let us, then, not fix our minds on
worldly things, which we cannot stay to enjoy,
but let us be concerned in erecting for ourselves
a mansion where time loses its power, and enjoy-
ment will be eternal. It is *sad, very sad*, for a
man to so give his time to self in this world
as to miss the way to his best and most lasting
home in the future.

Finally, Brethren, let us *forget* the faults of
our deceased Brother, and keep alive in our
memory only his many virtues and noble actions;
let us profit by the good example he gave us
while living, and keep his memory forever green.
May this loss of a Brother impress us with the
necessity of so conducting our own lives that
when it shall be our turn to leave this world,
we may die feeling at peace with all mankind
and our Maker.

W. C.—Let us pray:

O merciful and adorable God, who art the Resurrection
and the Life, in whom all shall live who believeth in Thee,
though they die, hear, we beseech Thee, the prayers of these
Thy servants assembled for the purpose of committing to the
earth the remains of our late Brother, whom Thou, in thy divine wisdom hast removed from our midst. Give us, O God,
whom Thou hast spared, a full knowledge of our helplessness
and dependence upon Thee, that we may meditate upon our
own mortality, and cease to neglect the many opportunities
of improvement in our lives which Thy goodness hath graciously afforded. Impress upon all present the uncertainty of
life, and the certainty of death. Look down, O God, bless
and comfort the disconsolate family, give them strength to

bear up under this great affliction, sustain them in their despouding moments, and so imbue their hearts with a spirit of resignation, that they may be able to say: "Not my will, but Thine, O Lord, be done."   Bless this Brotherhood, impress each with their duty to the other, give to our bodies health, and refresh our souls with the remembrance of Thee—the Bread of Life and the Fountain of every good.—Amen.

W. P.—The Brothers will now join in singing the FUNERAL ODE.

[At the conclusion of the singing of the Ode the officers will drop in the sprig of evergreen, and then the members, after which they may, at the discretion of the W. P., be disbanded; if so, the Marshall shall collect the Regalia, gloves, and other Lodge property.]

Funeral Ode.

Tune, "Hanover."

1. Our Broth-er is gone! his spir-it hath fled!
2. Let us who sur-vive, this king-dom pur-sue,
Hence-forth up-on earth he ranks with the dead;
Place all our de-light in things good and true;
But an-gels of mer-cy to meet him de-scend,
So fol-low the faith-ful, that we may ob-tain
And wel-come his en-trance to life with-out end.
A man-sion in glo-ry, and meet him a-gain!

Regalia of the Order.

MEMBERS—The "Knight of Garter," badge.

PAST PRESIDENTS.—A blue ribbon, 6 inches long from the bottom of the rosette to the fringe, and 2 inches wide, with "Knight of the Garter" badge at top, and emblem of office (a five-pointed star 2 inches across, with two gold tassels, 2 inches long,) pendant therefrom. Gold fringe at bottom from 1½ to 2 inches deep.

GRAND LODGE—Past President's badge.

GRAND LODGE OFFICERS.—St. George and Dragon in Garter, 1¾ inches in diameter, emblem of office at bottom, pendant from navy blue ribbon, 1¾ inches wide. Past Grand President, the same, with cross gavels at bottom and five-pointed star at top.

SUPREME LODGE OFFICERS.—St. George and Dragon in a Garter, 1¾ inches in diameter, with emblem of office at bottom and five-pointed star red enamel at top, on a triangle pendant from royal purple ribbon 2½ inches wide, stiff lining, stitched on both sides. Past Supreme President, the same as above, with St. George's cross in red enamel at top and cross gavels at bottom.

FUNERAL BADGE.

Black rosette, 3 inches in diameter, with black and white button 1¼ inches in diameter in centre, black ribbon, 2½ inches wide and 5 inches long from rosette to fringe, double silver fringe, one and a half inches long, name and number of Lodge and St. George and Dragon printed in silver.

INDEX.

	Page.
Officers of Subordinate Lodges,	2
Diagram of Lodge Room,	3
Ceremony of Opening Lodge,	4
Order of Business,	8, 29
Ceremony of Closing Lodge,	30
Installation,	32
Visitation,	37
Instituting New Lodges,	38
Funeral Ceremony,	41
Regalia of the Order,	46